To my dear friend Ruth Sanderson,
who always believed in this book.

—C. R.

To my daughter, Charlie.

—N. L.

ONLY MARGARET

A STORY ABOUT MARGARET WISE BROWN

written by
CANDICE RANSOM

illustrated by
NAN LAWSON

EERDMANS BOOKS FOR YOUNG READERS

GRAND RAPIDS, MICHIGAN

On May 23, 1910, a baby girl was born in Brooklyn, New York. That same day, a comet streaked silver across the sky. Halley's comet arrived only every seventy-five years or so.

The girl, named Margaret Wise Brown, slept as the star-flecked tail arced overhead like a fireworks show.

When Margaret was five, her family moved to a house on Long Island. Margaret hitched the neighbors' dogs to her sled and raced over the snow.

"Only Margaret would think of that," her family said.

Under hazy stars, Margaret spun stories on the sleeping porch. When she read fairy tales to her sister, she changed the words—sometimes scarier, sometimes more magical—like a genie spiraling from Aladdin's lamp.

At college in Virginia, Margaret once carried a rabbit
in a basket onto a train.

Another time she hired a taxi to drive her to Poughkeepsie,
New York. Six hundred miles in a cab!

"Only Margaret would do that," her classmates said.

Margaret's brother became an engineer.

Her sister studied physics.

Margaret had no idea what she
wanted to do.

When her essay was published in the
college magazine, her teacher urged her
to become a writer.

Margaret loved words but disliked commas.
Could she still be a writer?

She thought about
becoming a writer while selling
forks in a department store.

She thought about it as she
rowed a boat on a Maine lake.

At home she felt restless, like a pot simmering on the stove.

At last she moved to New York City, where she would meet other writers. The city, she hoped, would inspire her.

In a writing class, one of Margaret's stories began, "Jean came into the room and just sat down." Words, Margaret believed, should sparkle. Her words did not.

They just sat down.

Maybe she couldn't be a writer after all. She didn't have anything to say.

She switched to a teachers college, where she listened to children. The children's words sparkled. Their made-up stories seemed true as a new day.

Margaret decided not to be a teacher. She wouldn't write boring stories for adults, either. She would become a writer of books for young children.

"Only Margaret would make up her *own* job," her friends said.

Now Margaret moved through the world
in a new way.

She spied on spiders.

She watched a crow's wing slice the air.

She heard a mouse swallow.

Stories scrolled from her typewriter. Poems flowed from her pen. She wrote wrapped in raccoon robes. She wrote on scraps of envelopes. She wrote with her dog's nose propped on her toes.

She wrote a terrible story about a fairy bumblebee. Writing, Margaret found, was hard, like capturing fireflies in a jar. So she practiced her stories on children who listened and told her the truth.

One day an idea swirled around her. She grabbed it before it vanished and wrote about an old, old woman with a toothache, seventeen cats, and one little gray-blue kitten.

When the Wind Blew became Margaret's first book for children. With her check, she bought every bloom from a flower cart and threw a huge party.

"Only Margaret!" her guests said.

Then Margaret met a woman, a poet with the grand name of Michael Strange. They became very close. Michael Strange wrote big, important books for adults. Margaret only wrote little stories for children.

She worried that she should write important books for grown-ups, too. Maybe she only needed to think bigger thoughts, ask herself harder questions that she would figure out in her stories.

She wondered what made a spoon a spoon. She wondered what a shoe was really for. She wondered why snowflakes were shaped like stars.

Her answers became *The Important Book*. But it was not a book for adults. It was still a book for children. Yet Margaret was proud of it.

One night, Margaret dreamed of a green room and a red balloon and a picture of a cow jumping over the moon. The next morning, she reached for the notebook by her bed. Her pen sped, scrawling line after line about a bunny who named all the things in his room before he went to sleep. She didn't use a single comma.

That story became *Goodnight Moon*. Children everywhere fell asleep to Margaret's words, the wonder of great green rooms big in their dreams.

Other people were creating books for children, too.
But none had published over fifty books in nine years.
Margaret was famous.

She bicycled around Ireland through billows of mist,
glimpsing rabbits that made no sounds.

She drove slowly from Florida to New York so she could taste spring in different states. Just Margaret, seeing the world.

She worked on twenty books at once. She drove her pale-yellow roadster with the top down in winter, her Kerry Blue terrier beside her.

She surprised a group of traveling actors by arriving with a hot dog cart. Margaret sang made-up songs as she gave out hot dogs to the audience.

She went to parties and concerts and the theater. New York teemed with people and things to do. Yet in the middle of her busy life, Margaret sometimes felt the busy city rush by.

Lonely Margaret.

She bought a cottage on rocky Vinalhaven Island, off the coast of Maine. She called it the Only House, and there she lived like a cat, free to do nothing.

Content, she dabbed oils, painting pictures that pleased her. She washed her face in a basin under an apple tree. She saw the moon rise from a door that opened onto empty air ten feet above the ground.

Outside her window, Margaret could see tiny Starfish Island, where seals played and gulls nested. Sometimes she rowed to the island with her dog Smoke.

Mostly she watched waves and wind and foggy haze, hoping to understand the island's secrets. She wished she spoke another language, an island language.

Early one morning, she rose as stars faded, trading night for day. Sunlight poured over the little island. Gold flowed into the sea like a fireworks show.

Picking up her yellow notepad, Margaret wrote about lobster boats and whispering seaweed and a bat that woke an owl.

Inside the heart of her words, she learned the island's message. That everyone and everything is part of the world.

That she was not alone.

The Little Island became Margaret's next book, but her work was far from finished. Words about cats and rabbits and daisies and lazy porches and mysterious clock time whirled through her head.

She would write many more stories for children.
Books that could only be written by one extraordinary person.

Only Margaret.

AUTHOR'S NOTE

Margaret Wise Brown once wrote that she never meant to be an author of children's books. She called her career a "a happy accident." Yet she blazed a starry trail in the field of books for young children, a job most people did not take seriously at the time. Today she is recognized as a pioneer in the art of writing picture books.

Margaret was playful and fun-loving. She would tie lemons and oranges to a potted tree to fool people. She formed a club with two friends to celebrate Christmas whenever they wanted. She adored animals, especially dogs, though her Kerry Blue terriers were famously ill-mannered. Like many creative people, she also experienced periods of sadness and doubt.

The country always lifted her spirits, and she spent many summers on Vinalhaven Island off the coast of Maine. At the Only House—so named because she couldn't see the lights of any other houses—Margaret cooked and painted pictures and wandered in the nearby spruce woods. She also wrote stories at a desk that overlooked the green-blue, island-dotted waters of Hurricane Sound.

Her book *The Little Island* was awarded the 1947 Caldecott Medal for its illustrations by Leonard Weisgard, but she is best known for her classic picture book *Goodnight Moon*. Among the one hundred books published during her lifetime are *The Noisy Book, Wait Till the Moon Is Full, The Runaway Bunny, The Big Red Barn, The Little Fireman, Two Little Trains, Home for a Bunny, The Little Fur Family, The Important Book,* and *The Color Kittens.*

Margaret died in Nice, France, on November 13, 1952, after routine surgery. She was forty-two years old and engaged to be married. Her fiancé, a wealthy sailor, fell in love with the wild animal light in Margaret's greeny-blue eyes. He scattered Margaret's ashes into the sea at Vinalhaven Island. Inscribed on her tombstone at the Only House are lines from *The Little Island*:

*Nights and days came and passed
and summer and winter
and the sun and the wind
and the rain.
And it was good to be a little island
A part of the world
and a world of its own
all surrounded by the bright blue sea.*

Forty years after Margaret's death, dozens of unpublished manuscripts were found in a trunk in her younger sister's barn. Some of those manuscripts have been published, such as *The Daddies Are Coming Home*, *Goodnight Songs*, and *Wish Upon a Dream*. During her life, Margaret wrote some 800 pieces—stories, books, songs, and poems (including twenty-six books with "bunny" or "rabbit" in the title).

The world remembers her as the one-and-only Margaret Wise Brown. She gave the world her words, and generations of readers are grateful she did.

TIMELINE

1910	Margaret Wise Brown is born on May 23 in Greenpoint, Brooklyn, New York. She is the middle child of Robert and Maude Brown. Gratz is her older brother; Roberta is her younger sister.
1925	The Brown family goes to Maine for a summer vacation.
1926	Margaret and Roberta attend Dana Hall boarding school. Classmates nickname Margaret "Tim," because her hair was the same color as timothy grass.
1928–32	Margaret attends Hollins College in Virginia.
1934	She moves to New York City and takes a writing class at Columbia University. She mentally "lists" things in her bedroom in the mornings.
1935	She enters the Cooperative School for Student Teachers at 69 Bank Street as a teacher trainee. Classmates call her "Brownie."
1935	She writes a story, "Fifteen Bathtubs," which is published in *Another Here and Now Storybook* as part of the Bank Street teaching program.
1936	She moves to another apartment in Greenwich Village with a cat named Sneakers.
1937	Margaret's first book, *When the Wind Blew*, is accepted for publication. She spends the money she earns on flowers and throws a party to celebrate.
1937	She travels to England, France, and Ireland over the summer.
1937	She joins the Bank Street Writers Laboratory. She brings her new Kerry Blue dog, Smoke, to the Wednesday afternoon meetings.
1937–38	W. R. Scott forms a publishing company at 69 Bank Street, and hires Margaret as the editor.
1938	Margaret writes *Bumble Bugs and Elephants*. The artist she discovers, Clement Hurd, illustrates it. *Bumble Bugs* is published by W. R. Scott.
1938	She shares a house on Vinalhaven Island, Maine, that summer. She names a tiny island in the bay "Starfish Island."
1939	She writes *The Noisy Book*. Leonard Weisgard is the illustrator. Because the book is about a dog, Margaret gives him one of Smoke's puppies to use as a model.
1940	Margaret meets poet Michael Strange.

1941	She writes *The Runaway Bunny*, later illustrated by Clement Hurd.
1943	Margaret spends the summer on Vinalhaven Island at the Only House.
1943	She writes *A Child's Good Night Book* on an envelope.
1943	She moves to an apartment across the hall from Michael Strange.
1943	She rents Cobble Court, a tiny old house in the city, as a writing studio.
1944	Margaret's book, *Red Light, Green Light*, is published with illustrations by Leonard Weisgard. Margaret uses the name Golden MacDonald.
1945	Michael Strange gives Margaret a new Kerry Blue terrier, Crispin's Crispian.
1945	Margaret writes *Goodnight Moon* one morning. She calls her editor and reads it aloud to her.
1946	An article about Margaret Wise Brown is published in *Life* magazine.
1946	*The Little Island*, set on Margaret's "Starfish Island," is published with Leonard Weisgard's illustrations.
1947	Leonard Weisgard receives the Caldecott Medal for *The Little Island*.
1947	*Goodnight Moon* is published with illustrations by Clement Hurd.
1950	Michael Strange dies of leukemia.
1951	Margaret visits Cumberland Island, Georgia. She meets James Stillman Rockefeller Jr., and is soon engaged to marry him.
1952	She sails to France with Crispin's Crispian to promote the French edition of her book, *Mister Dog*. She is hospitalized in Nice, France, with abdominal pain.
1952	Margaret Wise Brown dies on November 13 from a blood clot after routine surgery.

A Partial List of Books
By Margaret Wise Brown

Big Red Barn. Illustrated by Rosella Hartman. W. R. Scott, 1956.

Bumble Bugs and Elephants. Illustrated by Clement Hurd. W. R. Scott, 1938.

A Child's Good Night Book. Illustrated by Jean Charlot. W. R. Scott, 1943.

The Color Kittens. Illustrated by Alice and Martin Provensen. Simon & Schuster, 1949.

The Fathers Are Coming Home. Illustrated by Stephen Savage. Margaret McElderry, 2010.

Four Fur Feet. Illustrated by Remy Charlip. W. R. Scott, 1961.

The Friendly Book. Illustrated by Garth Williams. Simon & Schuster, 1954.

Good Day, Good Night. Illustrated by Loren Long. HarperCollins, 2017.

Goodnight Moon. Illustrated by Clement Hurd. Harper, 1947.

Home for a Bunny. Illustrated by Garth Williams. Simon & Schuster, 1956.

A Home in the Barn. Illustrated by Jerry Pinkney. Harper, 2018.

The Important Book. Illustrated by Leonard Weisgard. Harper, 1949.

The Little Fireman. Illustrated by Esphyr Slobodkina. W. R. Scott, 1938.

Little Fur Family. Illustrated by Garth Williams. Harper, 1946.

The Little Island. Illustrated by Leonard Weisgard. Doubleday, 1946.

The Noisy Book. Illustrated by Leonard Weisgard. W. R. Scott, 1939.

North, South, East, West. Illustrated by Greg Pizzoli. Harper, 2017.

Red Light, Green Light. Illustrated by Leonard Weisgard. Doubleday, 1944.

The Runaway Bunny. Illustrated by Clement Hurd. Harper, 1942.

Sleepy ABC. Illustrated by Esphyr Slobodkina. Lothrop, Lee & Shepard, 1953.

Two Little Trains. Illustrated by Jean Charlot. W. R. Scott, 1949.

Wait Till the Moon Is Full. Illustrated by Garth Williams. Harper, 1948.

Wheel on the Chimney. Illustrated by Tibor Gergely. Lippincott, 1954.

When the Wind Blew. Illustrated by Rosalie Slocum. Harper, 1937.

SELECTED BIBLIOGRAPHY

Bader, Barbara. *American Picturebooks from Noah's Ark to the Beast Within*. New York: Macmillan, 1976.

Bliven, Bruce, Jr. "Child's Best Seller." *Life*. Dec. 2, 1946.

Blos, Joan W. *The Days Before Now: An autobiographical note by Margaret Wise Brown*. Illustrated by Thomas B. Allen. New York: Simon & Schuster, 1994.

Cech, John. *American Writers for Children, Vol. 22*. New York: Gale Research, 1983.

Gary, Amy. *In the Great Green Room: The Brilliant and Bold Life of Margaret Wise Brown*. New York: Flatiron, 2017.

Hurd, Clement. "Remembering Margaret Wise Brown." *The Horn Book*. Oct. 1983.

Marcus, Leonard S. *The Making of Goodnight Moon: A 50th Anniversary Retrospective*. New York: Harper, 1997.

Marcus, Leonard S. *Margaret Wise Brown: Awakened by the Moon*. New York: Harper Perennial, 2001.

Weisgard, Leonard. "Patchwork Memory." *Something About the Author: Autobiography Series, Vol. 19*. Detroit: Gale Research, 1995.

Text © 2021 Candice Ransom • Illustrations © 2021 Nan Lawson

Published in 2021 by Eerdmans Books for Young Readers,
an imprint of Wm. B. Eerdmans Publishing Co. • Grand Rapids, Michigan
www.eerdmans.com/youngreaders

29 28 27 26 25 24 23 22 21   1 2 3 4 5 6 7 8 9

Library of Congress Cataloging-in-Publication Data

Names: Ransom, Candice F., 1952- author. | Lawson, Nan, illustrator.
Title: Only Margaret : a story about Margaret Wise Brown / written by
    Candice Ransom ; illustrated by Nan Lawson.
Description: Grand Rapids, Michigan : Eerdmans Books for Young Readers,
    2021. | Includes bibliographical references. | Audience: Ages 5-9 |
    Summary: "This biography spotlights how Margaret Wise Brown's unique
    personality shaped her journey as a writer and pioneer of the
    picture-book form"— Provided by publisher.
Identifiers: LCCN 2021011532 | ISBN 9780802855084 (hardcover)
Subjects: LCSH: Brown, Margaret Wise, 1910-1952—Juvenile literature. |
    Authors, American—20th century—Biography—Juvenile literature. |
    Children's stories—Authorship—Juvenile literature.
Classification: LCC PS3503.R82184 Z86 2021 | DDC 813/.52 [B]—dc23
LC record available at https://lccn.loc.gov/2021011532

Illustrations created with digital materials

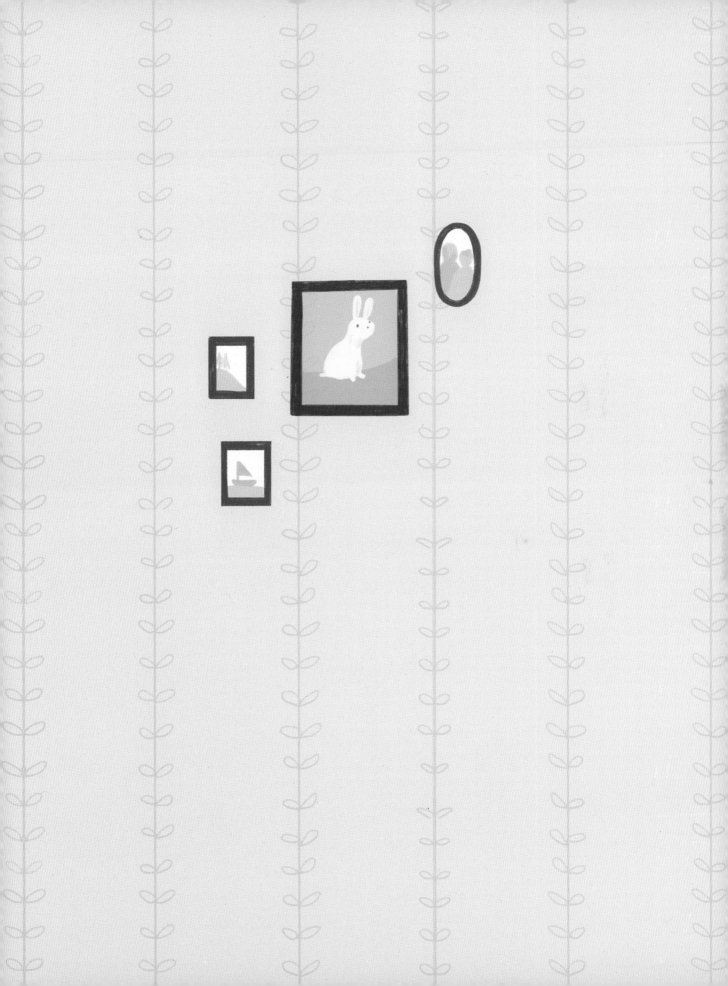